THE LAMB
A Passover Story

Michael J. Kurland

Illustrated by: Joel Ray Pellerin

To order additional copies of this book, contact:
Xlibris
1-888-795-4274
www.Xlibris.com
Orders@Xlibris.com

ISBN: 978-1-4797-8849-1 (sc)
ISBN: 978-1-4797-8850-7 (e)

Print information available on the last page

Rev. date: 05/29/2020

Dedicated to my parents,

Rob and Carol

The shepherds came our way today

And looked us over for quite some time.

They passed over every sheep and goat

And then their gaze caught mine.

I thought, "WOW!" They look so serious!

I wonder what this could be.

Foreheads poised and eyes intense

While they examined me.

With sighs of relief and hands upraised
In praise to the God Most High,
They made their choice and quickly came
For twilight was drawing nigh.

"Take this lamb for our Passover Meal,"
They shuffled quickly with their feet.
"KACH ET HA PESACH HA ZAY,"
They said, B'EEVREET.

I said, "I've been chosen!"
My heart thrilled with delight.
There must be something special
Taking place this holy night.

They gently led me on
And took me to their home.
I was the guest of honor,
Me and me alone.

My welcome was supreme,
Excitement filled the air.
I thought, "Even if I would die right now,
I wouldn't even care."

And then a light flashed from heaven, I knew tonight death would be my fate. But I trusted in my Kind Creator, for I knew He had made me great!

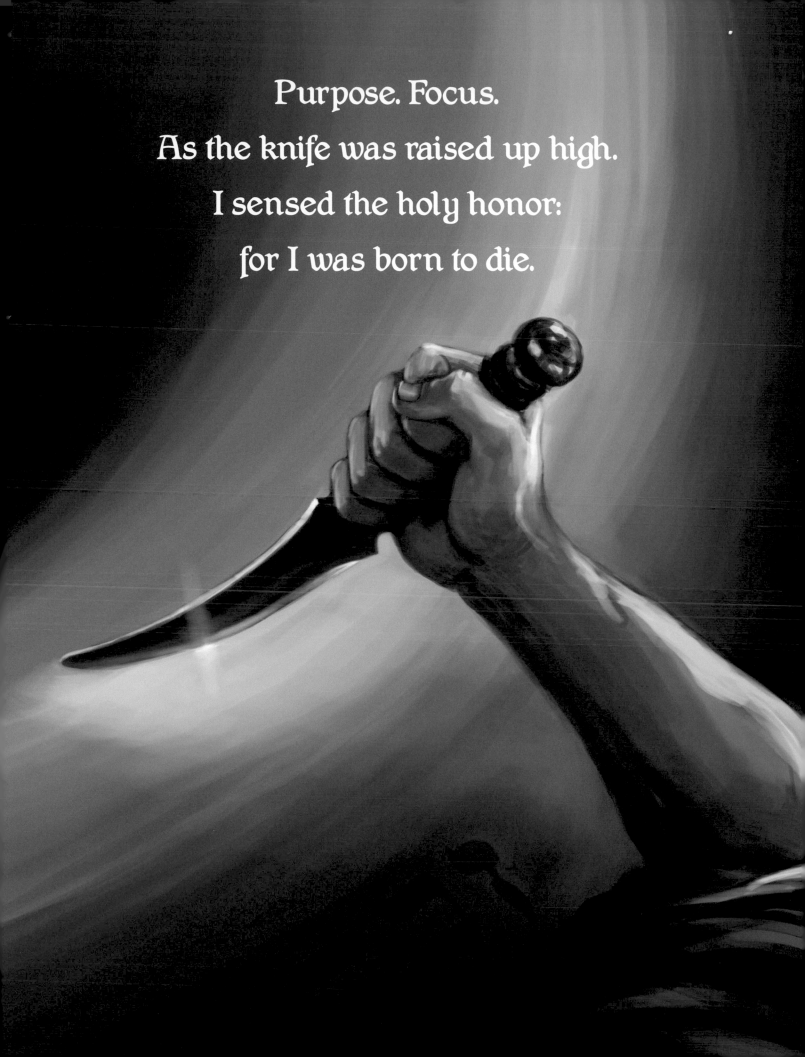

Purpose. Focus.
As the knife was raised up high.
I sensed the holy honor:
for I was born to die.

One last thought crossed my mind
Before the knife pierced through,
"I hope that they remember me,
Tonight and all year through."

HEBREW DICTIONARY
(For Hebrew word, please read from right to left)

BAKAR - 'to seek, inquire'. page 6

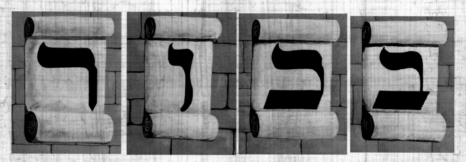

B' KOR - 'firstborn'. page 10

B'CHAR - 'chosen'. page 12

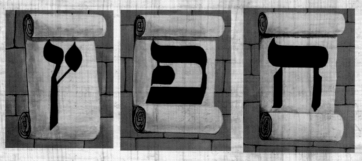

CHE'FETZ - 'delight in.' page 16

BA'TACH - 'trust'. page 18

ZAH'VACH - 'sacrifice'-male noun. page 19

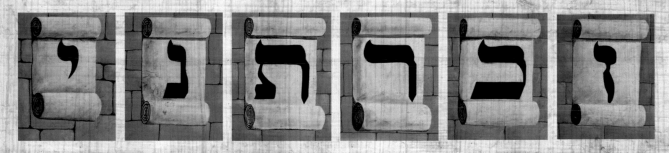

ZA'KAR'TA'NI - 'remember me'. page 20

Printed in the United States
By Bookmasters